The WARLORD'S PUPPETEERS

The WARLORD'S PUPPETEERS

Virginia Walton Pilegard

Illustrated by Nicolas Debon

PELICAN PUBLISHING COMPANY
Gretna 2003

To fifth-generation puppet master Yang Feng, friends
Chui Chu Tsang and Wang Qui Yue, and all
who share the gift of knowledge—V. W. P.

To Delphine—N. D.

*The word "Pelican" and the depiction of a pelican are trademarks
of Pelican Publishing Company, Inc., and are registered
in the U.S. Patent and Trademark Office.*

Library of Congress Cataloging-in-Publication Data

Pilegard, Virginia Walton.
  The warlord's puppeteers / Virginia Walton Pilegard ; illustrated by
Nicolas Debon.
    p. cm.
Summary: While traveling back to their warlord's palace in ancient
China, Chuan and the artist to whom he is apprenticed join a troupe of
puppeteers and Chuan learns about puppet proportions. Includes
instructions for making a simple sock puppet.
  ISBN 1-58980-077-X (hard cover : alk. paper)
  [1. Puppets—Fiction. 2. Ratio and proportion—Fiction. 3.
China—History—Fiction.] I. Debon, Nicolas, ill. II. Title.
  PZ7.P6283 Waqt 2003
  [E]—dc21

                        2002156419

Printed in Korea
Published by Pelican Publishing Company, Inc.
1000 Burmaster Street, Gretna, Louisiana 70053

The Warlord's Puppeteers

Many years ago in China, a boy named Chuan scurried through the marketplace in a bustling oasis on the edge of the desert. He dodged among the caravans from faraway countries that came to trade for the treasures of the Middle Kingdom. He and the artist to whom he was apprenticed had lived at the oasis for the long months of winter, saving money for their journey home. Now his arms carried the final supplies for their trip.

"Hurry!" shouted the artist the moment he saw Chuan. "A group of travelers is leaving this morning for the river near our warlord's palace." He snatched bags of rice, millet, and vegetables from Chuan's arms. "Hurry," he said again as he tucked the provisions among their belongings in a small cart.

The artist set off with long strides. "It is dangerous to travel alone," he called over his shoulder. "We do not want to be left behind."

Chuan followed, pushing the cart as quickly as he could without tipping it.

Among the travelers gathered at the gate, he recognized a troupe of puppeteers who had performed in the marketplace. The old puppet master and his young daughter were checking the harness that hitched their long-eared, gray donkey to a colorful, painted cart.

Chuan was fascinated by a carved trunk that sat on top of their load. Its scenes of fierce warlords on horseback dueling with swords made him long for the warlord's palace, where he and the artist once lived.

When the little band set out, Chuan angled his cart so that he could walk near the donkey cart to get a better look. "Tell me about your trunk," he asked the puppet master's daughter when they stopped to eat and refresh themselves.

"**I**t holds our puppets," the girl answered, in a voice so soft that Chuan had to lean forward to hear.

"Our family has been puppeteers for generations," said one of her older brothers, opening the trunk to allow Chuan to peek in. "My father buys only puppets made from the finest camphor wood. Each head takes the carver three months to create."

Chuan and his master became friends with the puppet troupe as they helped each other through the lonely, rough terrain. Some nights they stayed at monasteries along the route. Some nights they camped under the stars.

$\mathcal{E}$arly one morning, riders appeared over a ridge,
waving swords and shouting.
"Bandits!" cried the artist.

"Give us your valuables!" the bandits screamed. Their snorting horses reared and pranced, sending clouds of dust over the camp.

urprised and outnumbered, the travelers had no time to defend themselves. The bandits crammed everything of value into their saddlebags. They even tied the puppet trunk onto the donkey's back and drove him ahead of their horses when they rode away.

"We do not have provisions left to finish our journey," said the artist.

"Yes, but you can always make artwork to sell," said the puppet master. "I have lost my trunk of puppets. Now we have no way to make our living, and no money to buy more puppets."

They began to walk with slow, dragging steps. The puppet master's sons took turns shouldering the harness and pulling the donkey cart.

That evening, Chuan searched through their pack and found a green melon. He hollowed out its yellow flesh and began to carve.

When large eyes, a nose, and lips were recognizable,
he hurried to look for the puppeteer's daughter.
He found her seated, her head against her father's arm,
crying.

"Dry your tears and look at the puppet head I have made," Chuan said.

"The head is very cleverly crafted," the puppet master murmured, "but it is not the right size."

New tears glistened on his daughter's face.

Back at the artist's campfire, Chuan offered a bowl of slushy melon to his master. "Your new friends do not like your puppet?" the artist asked between bites.

C huan's face flushed with embarrassment. He felt a butterfly-light touch on his arm and turned to see that the girl had followed him.

"Perhaps this," she said, handing him a long, white radish.

The artist reached for the radish and smiled for the first time since the bandits had come. "Their puppets were this tall." He held his hand approximately two feet from the ground. "It is a rule that Chinese art must represent the true proportions of life. The melon is too big. The ratio of the head to the body must be one to six."

Chuan frowned, wondering about ratio. "The puppet's body should be six times the size of its head?"

"Yes, yes!" said the artist.

Chuan lay the melon aside and began to fashion a radish head with stick arms and legs.

Soon more puppets began to take shape from radishes and eggplants. Chuan and the artist walked by day and worked on their puppets each night by firelight. People donated scraps of bright fabric spared from their packs. The puppeteers consulted with Chuan and the artist to make a bald puppet for the funny master of ceremonies and other characters as well.

"When we come to the next town," the puppet master promised, "we will earn enough money with our puppet show to continue our journey."

One morning they were awakened by the sound of a donkey braying. Chuan raised his head to see the puppeteer's donkey dragging one broken slat of the carved trunk.

"Oh no!" cried the artist. "The bandits may be close behind."

Gathering their few belongings, the frightened travelers ran down the trail. The donkey trotted behind them.

The sight of a village in the distance brought shouts of joy from the little band.

"We will be safe from the bandits," Chuan panted.

"A perfect town for our puppet theater," the puppeteer's daughter said.

By evening, a makeshift stage had been built and a crowd had gathered. The puppets danced and talked and fought with swords in the hands of the skilled puppeteers. The bald puppet made everyone laugh with his jokes and silly antics.

During the performance, Chuan recognized a large man standing at the rear of the crowd. After the show, he pointed out the familiar figure to the artist, just as the man stepped forward.

"I have searched for you," the man said.

"We have such tales to tell you," Chuan and the artist answered. Their words tumbled together in their joy to see their protector, the warlord.

"Perhaps your stories would make good puppet plays," said the warlord. "I think my palace needs these puppeteers to perform for special occasions."

And so, the little group of travelers completed their journey in the company of the warlord, while they made plans to create elaborate puppets and stage many exciting plays.

You may have seen examples of Chinese rod puppets, shadow puppets, glove puppets, or string puppets such as Chuan and his friends made. During the Tang dynasty, puppets were used for religious instruction and for special occasions such as festivals, weddings, and funerals. Traveling troupes of puppeteers gave performances in marketplaces to earn their living.

To make your own puppet, turn a long tube sock inside out.
Tie a knot in the toe.
Turn the sock back right-side out.
Place a rubber band at the base of the knot, forming a head.
Draw the puppet's face.
Cut two small holes for your thumb and middle finger to stick out to make arms.
Push your pointing finger into the puppet's head for support.

What is the ratio of head to body?

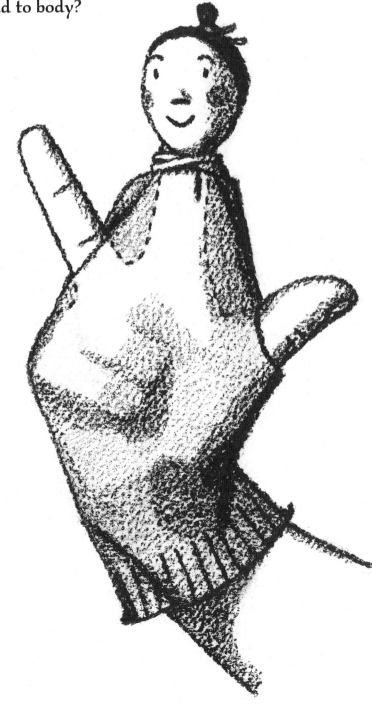